THE RELATIONSHIP RULES

Tips that matter more than others, whether it's a new or old romance

JONATHAN BROOKLYN

Table of contents

INTRODUCTION

As with everything in life, there are rules to follow. Applying these relationship rules can reduce the risk of injury. Relationship rules don't have to be boring and overwhelming. Love is made up of good and bad sides, and by the rules, you never go through the worst of a relationship. Pain and heartbreak are inevitable, but with the right relationship rules, love can be experienced like a bed of roses. It's not perfect, but it doesn't completely destroy or sabotage your mind. The point is that love is the most beautiful and extraordinary experience in the world, and the right relationship rules can help you achieve and live that dream love life. There are some relationship rules that can turn a driving relationship into a romantic relationship. Love is not as easy as it is portrayed in the movies because it takes constant effort and effort to make a relationship last. Not an effort that feels like work, but an effort that really makes you want to work. Using the right relationship rules will give you the wisdom to make your relationship work. Isn't it what everyone wants to prove that love can actually last a lifetime? Someone once said that falling in love should be easy. Sure, falling in love is easy, but staying in love takes a little effort. Without relationship rules, there is a lack of guidance and wisdom about the right and wrong ways to maintain a relationship. There is no one-size-fits-all approach to making a relationship last, but the majority often agree that these relationship rules are the right approach. Whether you seek a healthy relationship or keep it forever, rules can be beneficial in this situation. You may not realize it right away, but without rules, relationships can lack structure and direction. As a result, they become complacent and careless, and the relationship breaks down. Knowing the recommended relationship rules will help you better manage your relationships. And those involved will be happier too! Follow these rules in your own relationship, whether a new romance or an old one. As long as you're committed to building better relationships, what's the problem with creating magical experiences out of love?

CHAPTER ONE

Love your partner unconditionally

Do your best to love your partner unconditionally, even if it's hard to be selfish. The true definition of love is making someone as happy as you can, even if that means sacrificing some of your own happiness. Love means more than joy and sacrifice. Love your partner without expecting anything in return.

See it from your partner's perspective

Sometimes you get so focused on doing things from your own perspective that you forget to see things from your partner's point of view. Think about matters of the heart from your partner's perspective. Relationships are all about partnerships, and that partnership requires you to be open to theirs as well as your own.

End the argument immediately

As you learn these relationship rules, remember that love is a choice, not a decision. If you want your relationship to thrive and thrive, choose your partner rather than win the argument. There's no point in prolonging an argument if you end up losing your partner completely.

Make love regularly

Scheduling time for sex seems like a chore that starts to get boring. Sex should become an activity that both of you enjoy in order to become intimate and connect. It shouldn't feel like a routine, but it shouldn't be done often either. Find the right balance when making love with your partner.

CHAPTER TWO

Effective communication is the key to any working relationship

So if you really want your relationship to beat all odds, you need to learn how to communicate. Communicate with each other and grow together in love, but don't fall apart due to lack of communication over the years.

Give each other space

Couples often miss each other's health and give each other space to do their own thing. Learn to give each other space to be better individuals. Even the most intimate relationships sometimes need alone time to miss each other. Having space isn't a bad thing because it helps you love each other better when you get back together. Of course, there are still things like healthy space and too much space.

Don't take each other for granted

One of the most important relationship rules to remember is to never take your partner for granted. This is the easiest way to become a victim of problems and quarrels. If you don't appreciate their efforts and always assume they will always be there for you, you will create a lot of friction and conflict in your relationship.

White lies aren't bad

If necessary, tell a white lie, especially if it's a small lie that won't change your relationship but will make your partner happy. Of course, that's no excuse for making a habit of lying white *Tell her what she looks like in other dresses! That's all you say.

CHAPTER THREE

Don't hesitate to give positive criticism

Constructively speaking, it helps your partner become a better person. Don't be offended if they tell you something you can use to improve yourself. Remember that constructive criticism is a good thing, not something they say to disappoint you. Your partner may be right. You can use that feedback to grow. Is the lie comforting you or the truth offending you?

Always be there for them

If something happens to them, you are the person they should run to. Whether it's a good day or a bad day, please always be by my side. Hard times are the most frustrating part of a relationship. Stay with your partner and your love will shine brighter when the storm is over. This is one of the relationship rules to keep in mind. Because no one wants a partner who walks away when things get tough.

Show public affection, argue privately

Misunderstandings and conflicts should be discussed behind the door so as not to embarrass your partner. However, don't be afraid to express your love with simple gestures. Hold her hand, wrap her arms around her and kiss her!

Keep dating each other

Just because you've been together for years doesn't mean you have to stop dating. In fact, this is one of the relationship rules that keep your spark and chemistry alive. Remember to intentionally go on casual dates, not just when you have nothing else to do. Dating allows you to spend quality time with your partner without interruptions or distractions.

CHAPTER FOUR

Take care of yourself

Don't be lazy in your relationship. Just because you've been together for a long time doesn't mean you should stop looking attractive. Get those abs, work out, and do whatever it takes to maintain your attractiveness. Your physical features may not be the only reason they fell in love with you, but it plays a role.

Compliment your partner

Compliments are the best way to thank someone special for everything they do for you, no matter how small. It's simple, but it enhances their day and shows how much you love them. Effective enough to remind you.

Celebrate special occasions

Birthdays and anniversaries may come and go all too often, but it's those milestones that make memories. It's worth it. It's also a rare opportunity to appreciate everything your partner has done for you and to show them that they are the best thing that can happen to you. This is one of the most underrated relationship rules. Is as important as any other rule on this list.

Don't let your partner down

Don't intentionally make your partner feel bad or look bad. It leaves lasting scars that can damage relationships. The only thing you should do is pick them up and support them in any way you can. You can give constructive feedback, but don't deliberately attack their insecurities and weaknesses. Otherwise, you'd better be prepared to lose them.

CHAPTER FIVE

Learn to forgive

Forgiveness is one of the rules of relationships that should never be ignored. The key to a long-lasting relationship is to continue to forgive each other throughout the relationship. Stop harboring resentment, no matter how simple the tendency may be. Both of you should expect to make some mistakes during your relationship.

Respect your partner wholeheartedly

Respect is another relationship rule that people ignore. But respect is the foundation of trust and love. How can you expect to feel love if you don't trust your partner?

It's OK if your partner has other Praises

Your partner will have multiple crushes, even if they are committed to you — and that's fine. It's a tough idea, but if you can respect someone, so can your partner.

Trust your partner and your intuition

Trust is everything in a relationship. No relationship can work without genuine trust. However, you must also learn to trust your intuition when necessary. If something goes wrong, follow your intuition.

CHAPTER SIX

Don't talk about each other

It seems obvious, but many couples attack and punch each other in anger. This is what leads to toxic relationships, and why it is one of the most important relationship rules to follow. Do not complain or scold each other, even if you are tempted out of anger or frustration.

Always have a good time together

Quality time doesn't have to be exhausting or time-consuming. Sometimes it's as simple as a home-cooked dinner or doing errands together. Quality time is a way to make each other feel loved and rekindle the chemistry. Learn to spend quality time together. There is no better way to fall in love as the relationship grows.

Act like a child

Sometimes few pillow fights and cute wrestling matches won't hurt anyone. Not only is it fun, but it also helps you enjoy your relationship. Nothing feels better than having a pillow fight or laughing with your partner until you cry.

Be spontaneous with your affection

Love doesn't always wait for a special occasion or moment to express your love. Spontaneous surprises are always happier than planned surprises. It doesn't have to be Valentine's Day or an anniversary to give her a fancy dinner or a great gift. In fact, it feels great to be surprised on an ordinary day.

CHAPTER SEVEN

Stop Comparing

This is one of the important relationship rules, so pay close attention. No two relationships are ever the same, so stop comparing your relationships with other people. Instead of learning from other people's relationships, learn from the successes and failures of your own relationships.

Be their best friend

The best feeling is when your partner is not only the love of your life but also your best friend. Having friendships outside of a relationship avoids a lot of fights and conflicts.

Watch them say "I love you"

These three powerful words don't have to be said out loud all the time. You can say it in the form of gestures, quality time, physical contact, or even gifts. This is also known as the language of love. Everyone has different ways of expressing their affection, so be careful.

Don't make decisions when angry or upset

Our negative emotions are so powerful that they cloud our judgment and logic. One of the key rules of relationships is to never make decisions based on anger or frustration. Don't walk out that door, don't break up, and don’t curse. The more logical you feel, the more likely you are to regret everything.

Don't try to put yourself before your partner

As you follow these relationship rules, remember that relationships are always about partnerships and friendships and nothing else. You are neither better nor worse than your opponent. What you lack, others fill. Always keep this in mind before trying to control your partner.

Choose for each other every day

Just as love begins as an emotion, it develops into a decision. Relationships don't last long not because you're constantly feeling butterflies in your stomach, but because you're making a constant decision to love them every day. Even if they frustrate or annoy you, the choice is to make things work, not walk away just because things are hard. This is love.

CHAPTER EIGHT

Conclusion

Relationship rules don't exist to make relationships boring and rigid, they exist to make them more likely to last and be healthier. Without the right structure and guidance, there's no way to know if you're doing something right or wrong. You may push your partner away without knowing it. These relationship rules may seem simple, but following them can mean the difference between a romantic relationship and a failed one. They can turn neglect and complacency into romance and devotion.

www.ingramcontent.com/pod-product-compliance
Lightning Source LLC
LaVergne TN
LVHW052108160826
845678LV00015B/3432

* 9 7 9 8 8 4 8 5 3 3 0 5 7 *